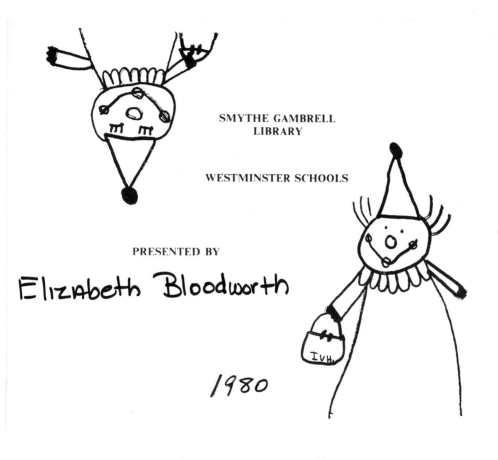

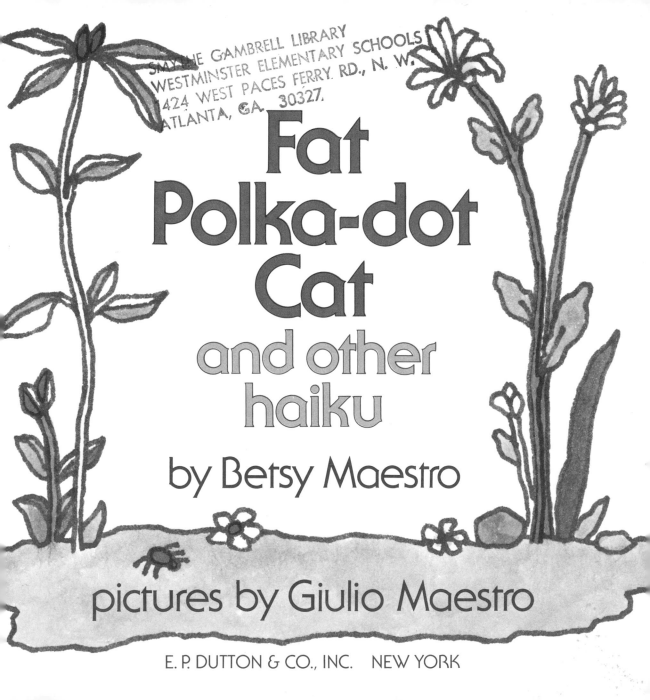

Fat Polka-dot Cat

and other haiku

by Betsy Maestro

pictures by Giulio Maestro

E. P. DUTTON & CO., INC.   NEW YORK

Text copyright ©1976 by Betsy Maestro
Illustrations copyright © 1976 by Giulio Maestro

Library of Congress Cataloging in Publication Data

Maestro, Betsy   Fat polka-dot cat and other haiku

SUMMARY: A collection of haiku depicting a variety of
scenes from nature.

1. Haiku, American. [1. Haiku.   2. Nature—Poetry]
I. Maestro, Giulio.   II. Title.
PZ8.3.M268Fat   811′.5′4   75-33641
ISBN 0-525-29625-5

Published simultaneously in Canada by Clarke,
Irwin & Company Limited, Toronto and Vancouver

Designed by Giulio Maestro
Printed in the U.S.A.
10 9 8 7 6 5 4 3 2

For Chang

Little ladybug,
Do you think our flowerpots
Are a real garden?

Raindrops like bubbles,
Clinging to each leaf like glue,
Even upside down.

Brown furry rabbit,
Its nose wiggly as jelly,
Is tasting clover.

Black and white kitten,
What could you be dreaming of
That makes your feet run?

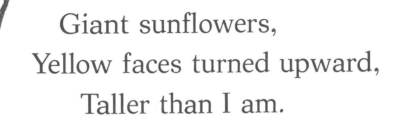

Giant sunflowers,
Yellow faces turned upward,
Taller than I am.

You greedy starlings,
Too busy squawking and now
Your breakfast is gone.

Tiny wildflowers
Scattered on the new grass look
Like leftover snow.

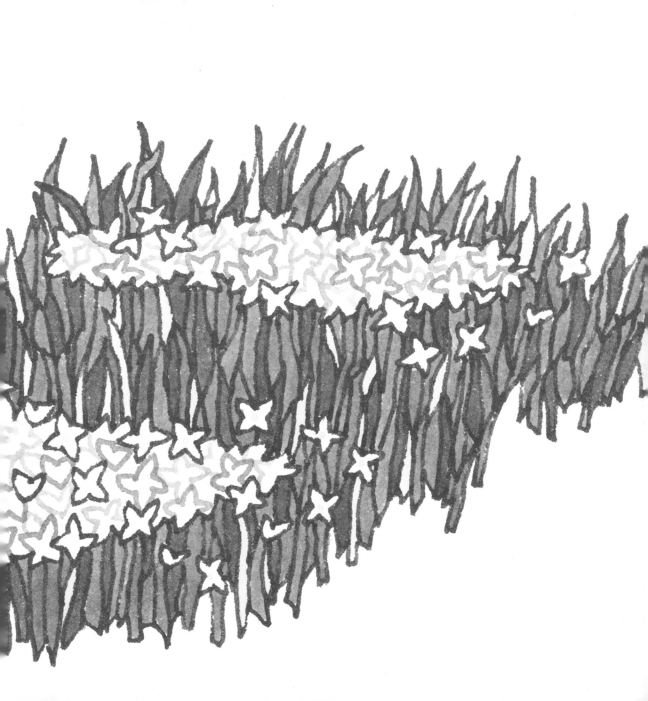

These flat stones are coins
Left from another time—stone
Quarters, pennies, dimes.

Quiet cardinal
Is like a bright red ribbon
In the snowy tree.

Some small smooth shells have
Spiral staircases inside,
Much too small to climb.

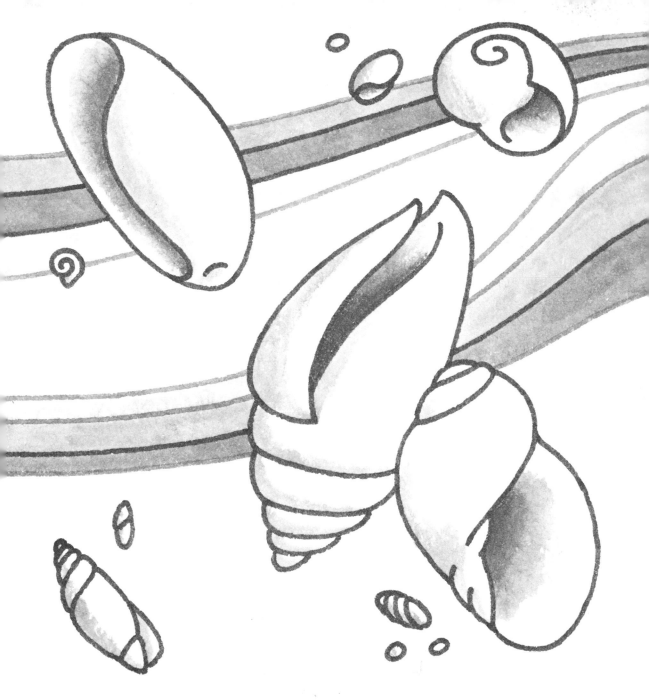

We ate a kumquat,
Planted a seed and waited.
Now we have a tree.

Three baby raccoons,
What busy fingers you have.
Into everything!

Fat polka-dot cat,
Did someone paint those spots on
To make you a clown?

Tiny chickadee,
How can you eat a hundred
Seeds without bursting?

Slow-moving turtle,
Why are you plodding uphill?
Down is much faster.